Etiquette for Success
Dining

TITLES IN THE SERIES

Etiquette for Success
Dining

Sarah Smith

MASON CREST

Mason Crest
450 Parkway Drive, Suite D
Broomall, Pennsylvania PA 19008
(866) MCP-BOOK (toll free)

First printing
9 8 7 6 5 4 3 2 1

ISBN: 978-1-4222-3970-4
Series ISBN: 978-1-4222-3969-8
ebook ISBN: 978-1-4222-7809-3

Printed and bound in the United States of America.

Library of Congress Cataloging-in-Publication Data

Names: Smith, Sarah (Freelance Writer), author.
Title: Dining / Sarah Smith.
Description: Broomall : Mason Crest, an imprint of National Highlights, Inc.,
  2018. | Series: Etiquette for success | Includes index.
Identifiers: LCCN 2018011614 (print) | LCCN 2018017318 (ebook) | ISBN
  9781422278093 (eBook) | ISBN 9781422239704 (hardback) | ISBN 9781422239698
  (series)
Subjects: LCSH: Table etiquette.
Classification: LCC BJ2041 (ebook) | LCC BJ2041 .S645 2018 (print) | DDC
  395.5/4--dc23
LC record available at https://lccn.loc.gov/2018011614

QR CODES AND LINKS TO THIRD-PARTY CONTENT

Contents

KEY ICONS TO LOOK FOR:

Words to Understand: These words with their easy-to-understand definitions will increase the reader's understanding of the text while building vocabulary skills.

Sidebars: This boxed material within the main text allows readers to build knowledge, gain insights, explore possibilities, and broaden their perspectives by weaving together additional information to provide realistic and holistic perspectives.

Educational Videos: Readers can view videos by scanning our QR codes, providing them with additional content to supplement the text. Examples include news coverage, moments in history, speeches, iconic sports moments, and much more!

Text-Dependent Questions: These questions send the reader back to the text for more careful attention to the evidence presented there.

Research Projects: Readers are pointed toward areas of further inquiry connected to each chapter. Suggestions are provided for projects that encourage deeper research and analysis.

Series Glossary of Key Terms: This back-of-the-book glossary contains terminology used throughout the series. Words found here increase the reader's ability to read and comprehend higher-level books and articles in this field.

Introduction

Dear Reader,

As you read on, you will learn that in any given situation you must be knowledgeable about the expectations set by society regarding your actions and how they will or will not meet the social norms for good manners and etiquette.

It being essential to your success, you learn how your behavior will always be central to how others see you. Unfortunately, many people are judged, or written off almost instantly because of their lack of etiquette.

Times have certainly changed, and while society adapts, you must set your own goals for politeness, good manners, and kindness. All around you there are modern dilemmas to face, but let your good manners set you apart. Start by showing sensitivity toward others, maintain a keen awareness about how those around you feel, and note how your behavior impacts your peers.

Consider that even with changes in the world around you, etiquette must be inclusive and understanding across ages and cultures, and sensitive to your setting. It is important that you take the time to learn; read, practice, and ask questions of those whom you respect. Learn about writing a business letter, sending holiday invitations, or communicating with peers— certain etiquettes should be followed. Is it rude to keep checking your phone during lunch with a friend? Are handwritten thank-you notes still necessary?

It is said that good manners open doors that even the best education cannot. Read on and learn what it takes to make a great first impression.

"No duty is more urgent than that of returning thanks."

"No matter who you are or what you do, your manners will have a direct impact on your professional and social success."

"Respect for ourselves guides our morals; respect for others guides our manners"

"Life is short, but there is always time enough for courtesy"

Words to Understand

famine: a very great shortage of food that affects many people over a wide area

foragers: members of a society who search for food for subsistence

gatherers: members of a society who gather foodstuffs for subsistence

Children who are encouraged to eat meals alongside friends and family from a young age will benefit by learning good social skills and table manners that they will remember for life.

Chapter One
The Importance of Good Etiquette When Dining Out or at Home

O f all the ways to relax, engage, and bond with others, sharing a meal may just be the most traditional and beloved method yet. Humans, after all, have been evolving for millions of years, and a lot of that change has come about because of changes seen in the way we obtain, raise, and ultimately share food.

Our earliest ancestors, for example, were mostly tribes of hunters, **gatherers**, and **foragers**. Food had to be found in the environment where people lived, whether that was forest, plains, or desert. Periods of **famine** and hunger were also common in ancient times. Because of the uncertainty of when the next meal would be and the nomadic nature of their way of life, efforts were combined and entire tribes of people worked together to share food and make sure that nothing went to waste.

But as time went on, our ancestors learned how to cultivate the earth, grow crops, domesticate livestock, and store and stock resources. This turn toward agriculture shaped the way our world is today, one in which most of us in Western society can eat fruit in the middle of a cold winter and enjoy grass-fed beef raised in fields thousands of miles away!

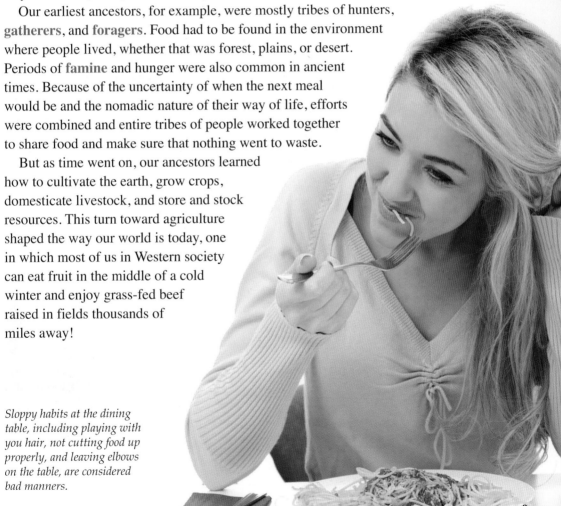

Sloppy habits at the dining table, including playing with you hair, not cutting food up properly, and leaving elbows on the table, are considered bad manners.

The Importance of Good Etiquette When Dining Out or at Home

Through all of this, however, food has remained very symbolic of important things like community, bonding, and social connection. Everything from religious services to long-heralded family traditions tend to center around the dining table. In fact, meals are probably a central component to many of your own greatest memories shared with your loved ones. And since dining together can play such a large role in the relationships and experiences you share with other people, it's helpful to be savvy and tactful when it comes to understanding all the ins and outs of proper dining etiquette.

This book will show you what it means to have proper etiquette when dining out or at home. You'll learn that showing consideration to your fellow dinner guests begins even

When dating in a restaurant, good table manners should be more rigid than they are when at home or with close family. Table manners are particularly important on a first date, as first impressions count.

Regardless of the situation, whether you are eating outside at a barbecue or in a classy restaurant, good manners should always be observed when socializing with friends and family.

before you sit down at the table, by understanding how to select a menu or place to eat with respect and fairness. You'll also learn about the many different dietary, cultural, and personal factors that come into play when deciding on what to eat, where to eat, and how to eat with your friends and loved ones.

The nitty gritty of proper dining rests on having good table manners. (Hint: you probably shouldn't rest your elbows on the table!) In this book, you'll be given a thorough and practical guide on how to eat politely, dress appropriately for the meal, treat other diners with respect, and set a table properly for the occasion, whether it's a formal luncheon or a backyard barbecue.

The Importance of Good Etiquette When Dining Out or at Home

Good dining etiquette is particularly vital during a business lunch, when a good impression is important.

If you're out in a restaurant, knowing how to treat the restaurant staff with respect is just as important as treating your fellow table mates with respect. This book will teach you how to order meals, appetizers, and drinks with tact, and how to handle sticky dining situations (like sending back food) with poise and courtesy.

Eating delicious food is just one part of the dining experience—the other part is the conversation you have while enjoying your meal. This book will give you some tips on how to improve your listening and communication skills, engage in relevant and polite conversation, and involve everyone at your table in a lively and pleasant discussion that serves to enhance the experience of a shared meal.

Lastly, you'll learn how to approach what can sometimes be the most awkward part of dining out: paying for the meal. From leaving the right tip to splitting the check, this book will show you that settling a bill doesn't have to be as uncomfortable as commercials and television shows often make it out to be.

So, whether you're eating dinner with your family, grabbing brunch with your closest friends, getting to know a date over a romantic meal, or taking an important client out for a business lunch, this book will help you approach each situation with poise, confidence, and class.

So let's raise our glasses, make a toast, and dig in!

Text-Dependent Questions

1. How did our earliest ancestors find their food?

2. Why is eating with company an important tradition?

3. Why is it important to treat your table mates with respect?

Research Project

Write an essay on why good etiquette when dining is important, regardless of when and where you are eating.

Words to Understand

breaking bread: to share a meal with someone (literary definition)

etiquette: the customary code of polite behavior in society or among members of a particular profession or group

patronize: to attend or go to a particular business as a paying customer, such as a store or restaurant

Breaking bread is a general term used to describe sharing a meal with others. In many countries, breaking bread is carried out in certain religious ceremonies. During marriages in some countries, bread is broken and then salt added, to symbolize health, long life, and wealth.

Chapter Two
Consideration for Others When Choosing a Menu or Restaurant Venue

Good **etiquette** is all about presenting yourself in a positive and polite way while also showing respect for others around you. It's about being considerate of other people's needs and at the same time respecting and honoring your own needs, too. For this reason, showing good etiquette when deciding where to have your meal is an important first step for a successful dining experience. In general, it shouldn't always be left up to one person to decide where to hold the meal, or, more broadly, what type of restaurant to **patronize**.

In other words, it's useful to take a little bit of time for planning beforehand to ensure that wherever—and whenever—you decide to enjoy a meal with your loved ones, it'll be somewhere that all members of your party can enjoy.

Where to Go? Some Questions to Consider When Selecting a Place to Eat

Options are endless when it comes to choosing a place to eat with your loved ones, family members, or colleagues. The following are a few questions you can ask yourself to help you make the right choice:

What Is the Tone of This Outing?

A more formal occasion, such as a business meal, should probably not be held at a loud bar. However, depending on the tone and intent of the meeting, you may not want to hold the lunch in a super fancy restaurant either. If, on the other hand, you're hoping to just relax and laugh with some friends, a restaurant or bar may be completely appropriate.

Here are some other suggestions for dining locales based on the intent and tone of your outing:

Home Cooking? How About Fine Dining?

According to data from the US Bureau of Labor Statistics, the average American eats out about four to five times per week. By comparison, the average Canadian eats out about two times per week, says the Canadian Restaurant Food Association.

Consideration for Others When Choosing a Menu or Restaurant Venue

Baby or bridal shower: casual dining restaurant with a private room to rent

First date: casual dining for dinner or lunch, or maybe a roadside diner (if you want to take a little pressure off!)

Family or friends get-together: family or chain restaurant for breakfast, lunch, or dinner

Bachelorette or bachelor party: restaurant or bar for brunch or cocktail hour, outdoor food festival or dining area

Informal lunch with colleagues: family or chain restaurant, healthy fast-food joint, food court, or coffee shop

When meeting for lunch with friends or colleagues, try to select an informal venue, where the dress code and ambience are likely to be relaxed and the staff easygoing.

Connecting People with Great Business

The popular website Yelp.com was founded in 2004. According to them, by mid-2017 Yelp users have written an astonishing 135 million reviews about businesses all over the world! Other useful online resources include Google Reviews and Facebook. Traditional resources such as the Michelin Guide and Zagat's are also accessible online.

How Much Am I Willing to Spend?

You'll learn more about the ins and outs of paying for meals in a subsequent chapter. But for now, just remember that you should be mindful of the overall cost of the restaurant. Going out to eat, while enjoyable, is still pretty expensive, even at cheaper fares. Why? Because if you think about it, the typical restaurant bill for one meal is comparable to a week's worth of groceries for many families.

Feel free to speak up if you don't feel comfortable going to a very expensive place. If money is tight, instead of saying, "I'm broke," try something more gracious that doesn't belittle your self-worth, such as, "I'd love to go out with you guys, but my budget is a little tight right now. Do you mind if we go somewhere a little less pricey?" Similarly, avoid saying anything that could be misconstrued as rude or resentful toward your friends, like, "You guys have way more money than me." Disparaging remarks like this can be hurtful and cause tension for everyone.

On the flip side, be considerate if your fellow diner expresses a desire to go somewhere a little less expensive, too. One way to get round this is to suggest two or three possible venues at opposite ends of the price spectrum when discussing where to go.

When looking for a restaurant to visit, be mindful of how large the check may end up being. Check prices online before you reserve a table to prevent an unwanted surprise at the end of the meal.

Consideration for Others When Choosing a Menu or Restaurant Venue

What Kind of Food Does This Restaurant Offer?

What type of food do you feel like eating? What about your friends? If you agree, then selecting the right genre of restaurant will be that much easier.

If you don't agree, try finding a place that offers a wide variety, and avoid places that stick to a specific niche. If you can check out the restaurant's menu online beforehand, all the better. Understanding what type of food the restaurant serves will be especially important if anyone in your group has certain dietary restrictions.

What Kind of Reviews and Reputation Does This Restaurant Have?

These days, people can post reviews of almost any business or establishment online. Feel free to do some research and check out the reviews to see what people are saying, but keep

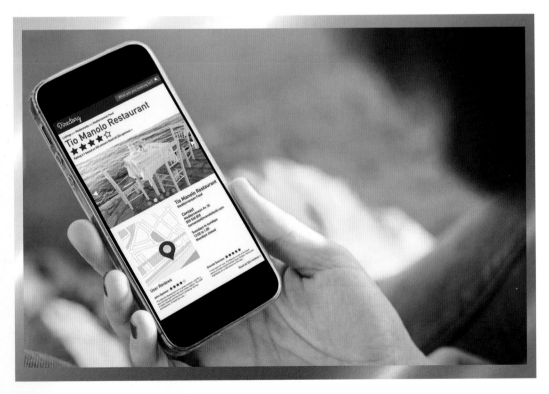

There are many ways to find out if a restaurant you haven't visited before is good. View websites and apps that include ratings and reviews by previous diners. Look for positive recent reviews and consistently high ratings—this is usually a good sign.

When choosing a restaurant, there are so many different types to choose from. Before making a reservation, ask the other members of your party what kinds of cuisine they prefer. This is very important, as some people can be very particular about what they like to eat. Making the mistake of choosing a restaurant genre that is unpopular with your fellow guests can cause a strained situation.

in mind that different people may have vastly different experiences at any restaurant, depending on factors like the individual server, the personality and mood of the diner, and the overall business of the night.

What Is the Most Convenient Time for Everyone to Meet?

You don't always have to wait until dinner time to eat with your friends! If people are busy in the evening with family and work obligations, consider meeting for a light breakfast before work or for a quick meal during lunch.

Consideration for Others When Choosing a Menu or Restaurant Venue

Be prepared to try something new! This Japanese chef has prepared a platter of sushi. Before making a reservation at this genre of restaurant, check with your party members that they like sushi. It is unlikely that a restaurant such as this one, will have many alternative choices on the menu.

Is Our Group Looking for Something New & Different or Tried & True?

The term **breaking bread** originally had its roots in a religious context. These days, it can more generally be used to describe sharing a meal with others. Sometimes, breaking bread with your loved ones in a time-honored and traditional way, such as attending a favorite restaurant, is the best route. In other situations, you and your loved ones may want to go somewhere new or try a type of food you've never had before. This can be a fun and simple way to take a little risk in life, so be sure to discuss this with your fellow diners beforehand. Lastly, when deciding on a restaurant to choose, be aware that it can sometimes feel like you're talking in circles. If you and your friends have a hard time choosing, try this tactic: suggest up to three restaurants and then let the group decide between these places. Sometimes, having fewer options actually makes it easier to choose. And if you're still struggling with the decision, then consider knocking your choices down to two!

Text-Dependent Questions

1. What does "breaking bread" mean?

2. What are two things to consider when trying to decide where to eat?

3. How often does the average American and the average Canadian eat out per week?

Research Project

Find a restaurant in your area that you'd love to try (you could also try a restaurant in another city or town that you've never been to but would love to visit). Then, go to http://www.yelp.com and see if there are any reviews listed there. Using this information, and anything else you can find out about the restaurant, write a one-page report on why you'd like to go to there and what type of outing you could see yourself having there (e.g., family meal, first date, etc.). What is it about the restaurant and/or the reviews that has helped you reach your decision?

Words to Understand

dietician: a person trained to give advice about diet and nutrition

faux pas: an embarrassing or tactless act or remark in a social situation

tactful: sensitive when dealing with others or with difficult issues

There are many reasons why people do not eat certain foods. They can be for religious, medical, ethical, or lifestyle reasons. Remember to respectful, tactful, and sympathetic to other people's dietary preferences.

Chapter Three
Considering
Other People's Dietary Requirements

These days, it seems like everywhere you look there are people with different dietary restrictions and requirements: vegetarian, vegan, Paleo, Whole30, gluten-free, sugar-free, low-carb, GMO-free, trans-fat-free, dairy-free, low-sodium, fat-free, and so on. For better or worse, these phrases have become important descriptors within modern-day food culture.

Keep in mind that "diet" has more than one meaning, and these may come into play when sharing a meal with friends and loved ones. On the one hand, a person who says he or she is "on a diet" is typically restricting or avoiding certain foods in order to effect some sort of physical change, such as weight loss or chronic disease management. For instance, a person with diabetes (a blood-sugar disorder) may follow a "diabetic diet" as recommended by their physician or **dietician**.

In a broader sense, however, a person's "diet" can simply refer to the kinds of food that someone habitually eats. There will be many factors that go into what a person does (and doesn't) eat, including religious, ethical, and personal beliefs, allergies, health conditions, and personal or lifestyle-related goals and activities. In this sense, everyone who comes to a table will be bringing along their own unique dietary preferences, even you. Successful dining experiences rely heavily on understanding and respecting this reality.

Eating Out "G-Free"

Gluten, which is a type of protein found in certain grains, has become pretty notorious in recent years. Many people have sensitivities or intolerances to gluten, and eating it can lead to a variety of uncomfortable symptoms: diarrhea, gas, and bloating. For this reason, many restaurants now offer gluten-free menu options. This list features forty popular chain restaurants in North America now offering "G-Free" options: https://glutenfreepassport.com/pages/fast-food-in-us-gluten-free-food-allergy

Tips for Eating Out Healthily

Top Five Don'ts When It Comes to Other People's Dietary & Food Choices

If a member of your dining party mentions that he or she has some dietary restrictions (either before the meal or at the meal), you can set a good example by being **tactful** and avoiding these **faux pas**:

1. Do NOT Ask the Person If They Have Any Diseases or Health Problems

Another person's health concerns are private, and in almost all cases none of your business. Be respectful and do not ask if something is "wrong" with them when they ask for a special menu or menu modification. If they want to tell you the reason behind their choice, they might—but if they don't want to tell you, that's fine, too.

You should also never assume or try to guess what's "wrong" with them either. Even if you are close with this person and are confident that they would discuss their issues with you, they may not want to discuss these things in front of other people at the table, or in a public place with strangers nearby.

2. Do NOT Tease the Person About What They Do or Don't Eat

A person has a right to eat what he or she wants without being made fun of for it. Show that you are a kind and thoughtful person by not teasing someone about where they want to go out to eat, what they choose from the menu, or what they need to ask the server about their food before placing an order.

3. Do NOT Try to "Tempt" the Person Into Breaking Their Personal Dietary Code

In addition to teasing someone for what they order, it's rude and impolite to try to "tempt" someone with the appetizers, meals, desserts, and drinks you order for yourself. Saying things like, "Come on, one bite won't kill you," or, "live a little," shows little respect for the other's person's discipline and conscious attempt to choose what's best for them.

4. Do NOT Make Someone Feel Guilty About Asking for What They Need

A lot of times, when we make try to make someone feel guilty for behaving a certain way, we're really just projecting our own guilt and discomfort about our own behavior. If you find yourself tempted to say something accusatory, rude, or condescending, then bite your tongue (no pun intended) and consider conducting a little self-reflection. What is it about this person's choices that is making you uncomfortable? Does it challenge any of your own ideas about food, health, body weight, body image, and self-worth? Keep an open mind and try to remember this helpful rule of thumb: *If you can't say anything nice, don't say anything at all.*

It is bad etiquette to pressure a member of your dining party to order something they are uncomfortable with. This is particularly important for those diners who are trying to use willpower to restrict their calorie intake for health reasons.

Most restaurants have plenty of options on the menu. Feel free to openly and honestly talk about what you would like to eat and what you would like to avoid. This will help your companions to understand your choices.

5. Do NOT Make a Big Deal Out of It

Whether you agree with a person's personal dietary choices doesn't really matter when it comes to trying to enjoy a nice evening out with friends, and what's on another person's plate or in their glass really shouldn't have any bearing on whether or not you all can enjoy your meal. If someone chooses not to order dessert or an alcoholic beverage, for example, resist the temptation to make some comment about it. Doing so is often thoughtless at best and mean-spirited at worst, especially since it's really not a big deal in the first place. Finally, if *you* are someone with specific dietary restrictions, then it's up to you to determine how much, if anything, you want to share about these restrictions with your fellow diners. You should feel free to openly and honestly talk about what you're eating (or avoiding) and why, but always keep in mind the ultimate purpose of the meal out: enjoying quality time together.

The dinner table is an inappropriate place to propose tips on weight loss or other dietary changes. Allow people to enjoy what they have ordered. Do not make comments about the sugar, salt, fat content etc. in a person's choice of meal, unless, of course, they decide to talk about it themselves.

Considering Other People's Dietary Requirements

Dining with one's friends and family is a wonderful experience that keeps everyone connected. In fact, meals are probably a central component to many of our own greatest memories shared with loved ones.

Though it may seem counterintuitive, the dinner table isn't usually a good place to discuss dietary changes, weight-loss tips, and so on. You could be inadvertently making other diners feel uncomfortable or defensive about their own food choices. Obviously, this can make you seem quite disrespectful, even if it's unintentional.

So always be aware of the tone and energy at the table. If people are asking you questions about the way you eat and seem genuinely interested and relaxed, then feel free to engage in a dietary discussion if you'd like. But if the conversation starts focusing too much on your food philosophy, if you start feeling like you're having to defend yourself, or if others seem to be growing a bit uncomfortable, then politely and lightheartedly redirect the conversation to another topic. Try saying something like, "I'd be happy to talk more about this later but I think we should get back to enjoying this delicious meal!"

Text-Dependent Questions

1. Explain the two most common definitions of the word "diet."

2. If someone at your table asks for a gluten-free menu, should you ask them a personal question about it, such as whether they have allergies or if they're trying to lose weight? Why or why not?

3. Why is it disrespectful to propose weight-loss tips to another diner during a meal out?

Research Project

Trying to stay lean and healthy but still want to go out with your friend? Write a one- to two-page essay on strategies you can use to make your next meal out a little bit healthier.

Words to Understand

bussers: people working in a restaurant who remove dirty dishes and reset tables

gesticulate: use gestures, especially dramatic ones, instead of or in addition to speaking, in order to emphasize one's words

manners: polite social behavior; a person's way of behaving toward and around others

Restaurant staff work hard to ensure your visit is a pleasant experience. Remember to be polite to your server.

Chapter Four
Good Eating Habits, Manners at the Table, Respect for Other Diners & Dress Code

There's an old saying that goes something like this: "Good grammar costs nothing," and the same can be said for **manners**. Appropriate manners are especially helpful at the dining table, where your polite and respectful behavior can really carry you far.

Of course, any expectations for your behavior will vary depending on the mood of the meal and the group of people you're dining with. Certain outings will undoubtedly call for more formal behavior and attire, while others will naturally allow for a much more relaxed and laid-back approach.

Some Basic Table Manner Rules That Always Apply Before & During Any Meal

No matter what the tone of your meal is—and whether it's out at a restaurant or hosted right in your very own dining room—there are a few general table manners that apply in virtually any mealtime situation, and for diners of any age.

Wash Your Hands Before Your Meal
This may seem like an obvious one but it bears repeating. You never know what kind of bacteria and germs get on your hands as you go about your day, and while the average person's immune system is healthy enough to fight off diseases and infections, good hygiene is just a smart habit to get into.

Sit in a Comfortable Position and Avoid Disrupting Others Too Much
If you **gesticulate** too much, speak too loudly, or

Wash your hands before eating or handling food.

fidget, you may end up knocking over items on the table or disrupt the people around you. Instead, sit comfortably and with a respectful posture in your chair. No, you don't have to sit ramrod straight, but you certainly should avoid putting your elbows on the table (forearms on the table are generally acceptable, however). You also should avoid tilting your chair back, slouching, hooking your arm over the back of the chair, or assuming any other posture that appears far too informal or irreverent. And if any food dish or item you need from the table is too far away, ask someone to pass it to you instead of reaching across the table and getting it yourself.

A table napkin is for removing small amounts of food from your lips and hands. It should not used for blowing your nose or wiping your face.

Keep Your Napkin in Your Lap

It's not impolite to use your napkin, but it *is* generally impolite to put it on the table or tuck it into your shirt. Instead, use your napkin as needed and always be sure to return it to your lap when you're not using it.

Don't Talk With Your Mouth Full

This is a huge no-no for several reasons. Speaking with a mouth full can make it difficult for other people to understand what you're saying. You may also be putting yourself at serious risk of choking on your food. Lastly, it's just plain unpleasant and obnoxious, and you may accidentally end up spitting food on someone.

Pleases and Thank-Yous Will Never Go Out of Style

Even if you're with your best friends who you can totally goof around with, you should still maintain the good habit of saying "Please" when you ask for something and "Thank you" when you receive it. It's a simple yet powerful way to show someone you respect them and have a good sense of self-awareness and sensitivity.

Don't Forget About the Restaurant Staff

Many people work together in a restaurant to make sure that the customers' dining experience is a success. If you've never worked in the service and hospitality industry, just trust that it's hard work! It's a great show of class and graciousness to express verbal thanks to the hostess, servers, food runners, **bussers**, and anyone else you interact with in the restaurant who is working so hard to make your meal enjoyable. If the food was particularly good, you can say to your waiter, "Give my compliments to the chef." He or she can relay this information to the chef, who is often overlooked, and the gesture is much appreciated.

Dress Appropriately for the Occasion

Whenever you go out in a social setting, you should dress in a way that feels comfortable and flattering. Keep in mind that restaurants are often chilly, so you may want to think about bringing a sweater or light jacket. You should avoid wearing outfits that are overly suggestive or inappropriate, especially on a first date. Other patrons within the restaurant (or even other people at your table) may be uncomfortable due to your provocative clothing, which may in turn make *you* uncomfortable, too.

Save the Grooming for the Bathroom

If you need to touch up your makeup, fix your hair, or get something out of your teeth that's

What Should I Do if I Notice Someone Has Something Stuck in Their Teeth?

While it can feel a little awkward, most people seem to appreciate being told when they have something stuck in their teeth. After all, nobody wants to walk around all day only to come home and see a huge piece of spinach stuck in their smile! If you notice a table mate has food stuck on her cheek or in her teeth, simply let her know. It's much better to politely inform her than to ignore it and pretend you don't see it.

gotten stuck, excuse yourself and head to the bathroom. It's impolite to do these sorts of things at the table. The same goes for moments when you suddenly are stricken with a coughing or sneezing fit. Be sure to wash your hands before returning to the table.

Watch your Volume and Language

The noise inside a restaurant can get loud sometimes. But if you're speaking too loudly to your friends, other diners around you may have a hard time communicating with their own party (plus, you may end up getting eavesdropped on). To make sure you can hear and be heard, make eye contact with the person or people you're speaking to and be sure not to interrupt or talk over someone else at the table. You should also be aware of the language you use and the things you discuss. Curse words and inappropriate topics may disrupt other diners near you, especially if you're speaking loudly (and especially if they have young children with them). You have a right to talk however you choose with your closest companions but try to save the saltiest convos for more private settings.

Don't Stack Your Plates

While you may think you're helping the wait staff, scraping and stacking together your plates when you're done eating could actually cause more harm than good. Many restaurants have a policy that prohibit servers from plate stacking, which could get them in trouble if you make it appear as if they've done so. Instead, understand that servers are professionals and know how to

Dinner Manners in a Formal Setting

properly collect and carry used dishes from your table. Sit back, let them do what works for them, and be sure to thank them for the help.

A Few Etiquette Rules for Specific Dining Occasions

Business Luncheons, Weddings, and Other Formal Occasions
- Don't sit down or place your napkin in your lap until your host has done so.
- At formal table settings with multiple plates and silverware, the general rule of thumb is to "start from the outside in." That is, the fork furthest away from the plate is the salad fork, the next is the dinner fork, and so on.
- When you're done with your meal, leave your plate where it is and put your fork and knife on the plate, either in a "20 minutes past 4 o'clock" position (if you imagine the plate as a face of a clock), or in the middle lying side by side with the sharp blade of the knife turned inward.
- Leave your napkin on your lap until you leave the table, at which point you may loosely fold it and place it to the left of your plate.
- When in doubt, follow the lead of your host, hostess, knowledgeable table mate, or wait staff.

First dates
- Don't drink too much alcohol. You may think that having an adult beverage can help calm your nerves, but if you drink too much you may end up doing or saying something that you'll later regret, or which doesn't paint you in your best light.

Good Eating Habits, Manners at the Table, Respect for Other Diners & Dress Code

- Don't use your phone at the table (this applies for almost all settings). To avoid temptation, leave your phone on silent and keep it in your pocket or purse. Pay attention to your date instead—after all, you're there to get to know him or her, aren't you?
- Show up on time! If anything, be a little bit early, especially if you've made a reservation.

Buffets, Barbecues, Clambakes & Meals at Friends' Houses

- Find out beforehand if you're expected to bring something, such as a side dish or dessert. Even if the host or hostess insists that you don't need to bring any food or beverages, you should still plan on showing up with some sort of gift, such as a thank-you card, a potted plant, or a nice bottle of wine. Small gestures like this go a long way.

When taking food from a buffet, take a little to start with. If you realize you don't like something you've taken, don't put it back, even if it is uneaten. Only go back for second helpings once everyone has been served.

- In all settings, but especially when at someone's home, it's impolite to complain about the food. If there's something you don't like, simply leave it on your plate, and unless you have specific dietary or personal reasons for not eating it, at least give it a try first.
- Offer your help to the host or hostess before, during, or after the dinner. It's a wonderful way to express your gratitude for the meal beyond just saying thank you (which is still appreciated and important).
- Do not go for second helpings until you're sure that everyone in attendance has already had their share.
- Avoid going overboard on food and drink in general. This will help you stay comfortable, enjoy what you're eating, and avoid feeling too full or becoming intoxicated. That old adage of "everything in moderation" also applies at all-you-can-eat buffets!
- Be friendly. Introduce yourself to guests you don't know.
- Send a note of thanks in the day or two after the dinner party.

Text-Dependent Questions

1. Should you stack your plates for the waiter or waitress when you're done with your meal? Why or why not?

2. If you're at a formal dinner and there are multiple forks at your table setting, which one do you use first?

3. Give three examples of basic table manners.

Research Project

Using what you have learned from reading this chapter, host a formal dinner with your family or friends. Have fun with it! Feel free to dress up, help your parents cook an elegant meal, or even playact being a waitress or waiter. Then write a one-page essay about your experience. How did it feel to share a meal in such a formal way? What did you like about the meal with your loved ones? What would you do differently next time?

Words to Understand

antiquated: old-fashioned or outdated

inarticulate: lacking the ability to speak fluently and coherently

sommeliers: professional wine experts

Popular restaurants get very busy, particularly at peak times. While it is customary to expect good service, try to exercise a little patience while waiting to be served if the restaurant is very full.

Chapter Five
Ordering Food & Drinks

So you've decided with your friends where you should go to enjoy a nice meal out. Perhaps you're celebrating something, or simply looking to spend some quality time with people you love. You've dressed appropriately and fashionably for the occasion, you've shown up on time, and you're ready to take a look at the menu and decide on your meal.

Now, how do you actually go about ordering the food in the first place?

First Things First: Is It Waiter, Waitress, or Server?

Depending on what year you were born, you probably have never heard the term "stewardess" before. This **antiquated** term used to be used to describe flight attendants, an occupation that used to be exclusively female.

These days, "stewardess" is considered sexist. In the same vein, many people feel that using the term "waitress" is sexist as well. Whether you agree with this or not, it's not a bad idea to stick to the term "server" when referring to the staff member who is attending you and your party. It's generally acceptable to refer to a female server as a "waiter," too. And even though you probably won't be shunned if you use the term "waitress," you may want to get in the habit of using a more neutral and socially acceptable term.

Of course, an even better idea than referring to your server as waiter or waitress is referring to them by their first name. Servers may be wearing nametags, or will at least introduce

With good etiquette, eating out can be great fun!

Ordering Food & Drinks

Read all of the menu before ordering. Make sure the other diners at your table have chosen their meal before you signal to the server that you are ready to order.

themselves to you when they first approach the table. Calling your waiter by their first name is respectful and will probably make it easier for you to catch their attention if you need it (rather than simply yelling out, "Excuse me, waitress!" which is a huge social faux pas).

Helpful Things to Consider When Ordering Food & Drinks

Read the Full Menu
The chef and rest of the restaurant staff put a lot of time and effort into crafting their menu. While there's nothing wrong with always ordering the same thing, you may want to consider looking through the whole menu and trying something new every once in a while.

Of course, you shouldn't hem and haw over what you're going to get either. Waiting too long to decide can frustrate your fellow diners, who may be starving and ready to eat!

When your food does arrive, wait to dig in until everyone has their plate in front of them. Be sure to take a few moments to simply observe, smell, and appreciate the presentation, too. And you'll get much more enjoyment out of your meal if you eat slowly, take small bites, and don't rush.

Ask Questions

If you're not sure about an item on the menu, ask your server for more information. Restaurant staff, including waiters, **sommeliers**, and your hosts and hostesses, know a lot about the food and drinks on the menu.

Asking questions is especially important if you're traveling abroad or are at an ethnic establishment, such as an Asian, Greek, French, or Indian restaurant, where you may not know much at all about the culture's unique foods and customs. You may not even know how to use certain utensils (such as chopsticks), so feel free to ask for advice.

You shouldn't be ashamed about not knowing what something on the menu means. You're there to enjoy your meal, not be a master chef. By asking questions, you may end up learning something interesting about food and discovering a new favorite dish. So ask away!

What to Do If You're Waiting Too Long for the Waiter

Going out to eat should be fun, and nobody wants to experience slow service. If you find yourself waiting a long time for your server, it's important to remain easygoing, kindhearted, and calm. Consider giving the waiter the benefit of the doubt: maybe there's a hold-up in the kitchen or maybe he or she suddenly has to cover for another server. Even if your service is slow because the waiter is incompetent or simply not doing his job well, you should still remain polite.

Avoid Using Filler Words Such As "Um," "Ah," or "Like"

There is virtually no situation in which your speech will be improved or your message more clearly shared if you use words such as "um," "ah," or "like." Saying filler words like this can make you sound **inarticulate**, unintelligent, and unsure of yourself. Understandably, it's especially important to avoid these words if you're out on a business lunch with other coworkers, clients, or your employers.

You should also keep in mind that your waiter is likely quite busy. He or she may have many other tables waiting for service, so don't waste your time, your server's time, or your

friends' time by saying a lot of ums when asked what you would like to order. If you really haven't decided, simply say something such as, "Please come back to me."

Of course, this can be a very difficult habit to break. Just do your best, act confidently, and don't be too hard on yourself if you slip up.

Stop Eating When You've Had Enough

Listen, you're a young adult now. There's no such thing as a "clean plate club" when it comes to dining out with friends. So don't keep eating all of your food simply because it's there. If you're full, then stop. You can always offer some of your food to your dinner date, ask for a to-go container, or just leave it on your plate.

To Share or Not to Share?

For various reasons, some diners opt to share one dish between two people. There's no hard and fast rule about how socially acceptable this is. Some restaurants frown upon it, while others don't mind at all as long as you're a paying customer. But keep in mind that some restaurants may add a small fee for split dishes and that it may be easier on the serving staff to simply ask for an extra spoon, fork, or

Always have a glass of water with your meal. Not only does it aid digestion but it will also make you feel fuller so that you don't overeat.

plate, rather than asking them to separate the meal for you back in the kitchen. Consider asking to be seated at the bar if the restaurant is very crowded and you know you and your dinner date will only be ordering some drinks, a few appetizers, or a shared meal.

Keep Your Water Glass Full

Drink water throughout your meal, especially if you're drinking alcoholic beverages, too. Why? It can prevent you from overeating, keep you from consuming too much alcohol, help you stay hydrated, and aid with digestion. If your waiter comes around and refills your water glass for you, remember to pause and say thank you before resuming your meal and conversations.

Many restaurants serve large portions. Don't feel that you need to eat everything served up.

Ordering Food & Drinks

Before making a reservation, check the restaurant's opening and closing times. Try not to arrive late as staff may be under pressure to finish up and close before you are ready to leave. This may then ruin your dining experience. Likewise, arriving early can also cause issues, especially if your table is not yet ready.

Take Your Time Enjoying Your Meal but Don't Overstay Your Welcome

When you go to a restaurant, you have every right to be there just as much as any other paying customer, even if other tables buy more food and spend more money. So don't feel like you should rush your meal simply because you "only" ordered a main course but no appetizer, or food and no drinks. Eating out is a pleasant experience, made even more pleasant by being able to relax with your loved ones.

That said, it's polite to stay mindful of how busy the restaurant is, how many people are in your party, and how long you've been taking with your meal. As mentioned, if you're planning on only having a few drinks and an appetizer, try getting a spot at the bar so another party can benefit from the use of a table. And if you arrive at a restaurant close to closing time, try not to order the most complicated item on the menu or linger after your meal is over.

Text-Dependent Questions

1. What term or terms do most people find acceptable to use for the restaurant staff member who takes your order?

2. Give two or three valid reasons why you may ask to send your food back to the kitchen.

3. What are the benefits of drinking water throughout your meal?

Research Project

Do an online search for ethnic restaurants in your area that list their menus online. Take a look through the different menus and identify two or three dishes that you've never had before, or which contain ingredients you've never heard of. Do some research about this food and culture (better yet, go to the restaurant and order the dish you're interested in!) then write a one- to two-page report about what you've learned.

Even with today's communication-technology overload, the face-to-face business lunch is still an important way to build relationships with potential new business partners.

Chapter Six
Making Polite & Relevant Conversation

Meals out with your friends, loved ones, colleagues, or clients are about enjoying great food. These meals are *also* about developing strong bonds and sharing positive social connections with the people in your personal and professional lives. One of the most important things you can do to help ensure that this sense of shared connection is felt by everyone is by communicating well with all of the people at your dinner party.

At the heart of communication lies verbal and nonverbal communication. Verbal communication consists of the words you use. Nonverbal communication includes things like the tone of your voice, the posture and movement of your body, your facial expressions, and eye contact. A good communicator needs to use both her verbal and nonverbal communication skills well in order to put her point across, share her beliefs, and express herself respectfully throughout all types of discussions.

A good communicator, however, is also a good listener. Research shows that being a good listener, and being seen by others as a good listener, can even improve a person's job performance, social interactions, and relationships. And since having good etiquette (at the dining table and elsewhere) is all about presenting yourself to others in the best and most honorable way possible, no discussion about dining etiquette would be complete without talking about . . . well, . . . talking.

A Quotation to Ponder
"Most people do not listen with the intent to understand; they listen with the intent to reply."
—American author and speaker Stephen R. Covey

Good conversation is as central to a successful dining-out experience as good food. Diners must have interesting things to say and be good listeners too.

When families and friends dine together, it is a wonderful way to enjoy a relaxed and memorable occasion with interesting conversation. In fact, in the busy world we live in today, dining together is one of the few opportunities that families have to spend time in each others' company during a busy week.

Top Tips on Being an Active Listener

You might not think of listening as a skill. In fact, many people seem to **take for granted** the fact that we are born with ears for listening, brains for comprehending, and mouths for speaking. But there are several things you can do to break old conversational habits and become better at listening. Here are a few suggestions from the company SpunOut.ie to get you started:

- **Ask open-ended questions.** Such as ones that center around information concerning *how*, *who*, *where*, *what*, *when*, and *why*. These questions (as opposed to simple yes/no questions) show your table mates that you're interested, and help keep the conversation going so you can hopefully avoid those awkward silences.

- **Summarize what the person says before asking more questions.** This helps both you and the other person make sure that you are being understood and establishes the important fact that, yes, you've actually been listening.

- **Repeat words or phrases that the person uses.** This can stimulate further reflection and garner more insight from the other person, which helps keep the conversation moving forward.

- **Clarify things you're not sure about**. If you're not sure about something, repeating what the person said and prefacing it with the phrase, "This is what I'm hearing," can help make sure that you're understanding the person well. But if that doesn't work, you can try saying something like, "Tell me more about that." Don't assume you understand

Dining out in a restaurant is an excellent and romantic way to get to know a new partner. The ambience created by the setting is very often the perfect way to get to know someone better.

if you're not sure, especially if the restaurant you're in is loud and you're having a hard time hearing.

- **Use encouraging verbal and nonverbal communication.** Use supportive words and friendly body language to show the other person that they should feel safe and comfortable talking to you.

- **React with compassion.** If someone is sharing a difficult personal story, whether over a meal or somewhere else, it's good etiquette to react with compassion and kindness. Saying something like, "How can I help?," "That's so interesting," or "That must be hard," can really help validate a person's feelings. Not only will this help them feel more comfortable talking to you but it can also help them gain greater insight into their own struggles and stories.

Eating together is an important aspect of family life. It teaches children good table manners and also the art of conservation, which is vital to their all-round education.

Having an argument or a heated discussion is not appropriate in a restaurant. Other diners do not want to hear what you have to say or endure raised voices.

Some Dos & Don'ts of Conversations During a Meal

DO Ask Questions About Things You're Interested In and Things That Are Appropriate to Discuss Over a Meal

Feel free to explore topics of discussion with your friends that are **relevant** to the context of the dining table. As mentioned earlier, you should probably avoid conversations about dieting and weight loss. Topics that are graphic or grotesque in nature, or things that are considered "hot-button" topics, like politics, religion, and finances, are likely not appropriate to discuss over a meal, depending on the tone and familiarity of the group. Be savvy and self-aware enough to steer the conversation back to safe ground if you notice things running awry.

Making Polite & Relevant Conversation

When dining in a group, let the other diners have their chance to speak. Listen to what they have to say. Don't interrupt and avoid the temptation of always bringing the conversation back to you.

DO Make Eye Contact With the Person Who's Talking

Listening quietly and looking at the speaker is respectful, as is gently nodding and offering brief words of encouragement, such as, "Go on," or "Interesting." Avoid interjecting too often though, as this could be misconstrued as interrupting.

Lastly, DON'T Interrupt!

When someone is talking, let them talk. Practice your **active listening** skills, and try to interject when you feel it's appropriate.

DON'T Hog the Conversation

Let other people speak, and avoid the temptation to always bring a discussion back to you.

Text-Dependent Questions

1. What does it mean to be an active listener?

2. Name two ways to be an active listener.

3. Are "hot-button" topics always appropriate to discuss at the table? Why or why not?

Research Project

Pretend that you are going out on a first date. Come up with between fifteen and twenty questions you could ask your new date that might stimulate an interesting conversation and help you get to know the person.

Words to Understand

social norm: rules of behavior that are considered acceptable in a group or society

tab: bill or invoice; money owed

tip: a sum of money given to someone as a reward for their services

Not all places will accept all forms of payment (cash, credit, etc.). If in doubt, ask before ordering.

Chapter Seven
Settling the Check & Tipping

In this day and age, more and more people are going out to eat. Whether takeout, fast food, casual restaurants, or fine dining, people across North America are enjoying and sharing meals outside of the home.

Who's Buying? General Guidelines on Who Pays the Check

So who pays for the delicious meal? Here are a few helpful suggestions:

- If it's a business lunch to which you were invited, the expectation is that whoever invited you will pay. If *you* invited the other person then you should pay.
- If you're among a group of friends there is usually a bit more flexibility. For instance, you may still want to offer to pay, especially if you did the inviting. You can also choose to split the check instead: either evenly between the number of people present or divided based on who ordered what. Do what you're comfortable with, and if you feel like you are being forced to pay more than you want then politely speak up.
- No, the man does *not* have to always pay for the meal. It's perfectly acceptable to split the bill on a date or to expect that whoever asked the other person out should pay.

Is Eating Out the New Norm?

Between 2015 and 2016, American people spent *more* money on restaurants and bars ($54.9 billion) than they did on groceries ($52.5 billion). This was the first time that the US Bureau of Labor Statistics had ever recorded that. Experts say that this trend shows that going out to eat is being seen as less of a luxury and more of a way of life.

But out of all the aspects of going out to eat with friends, perhaps the one that causes the most discomfort and anxiety is figuring out how to pay the **tab**. And, as it turns out, this may be the one area that requires the most good etiquette and poise. Why? Because knowing how to settle the check graciously can help ease the minds of your other dining guests, and help you come off as fair, tactful, and considerate.

Settling the Check & Tipping

How to Split the Check in a Restaurant

- Of course, if someone insists on paying for you (whether because they feel they owe you a favor, because the dinner is held in your honor, or because they are simply acting out of kindness) then accept graciously.
- Many groups of friends or couples prefer to alternate who pays for the meal every time they go out. This can work well, too; especially if you go out regularly.

Some "Tips" on Tipping Tactfully

Different situations, and sometimes different meals, come with different tipping norms. Indeed, in some cultures, tipping is frowned upon or even prohibited. In others, such as the United States and Canada, tipping is customary and a vital part of the server's wage (the main difference being that restaurant staff in Canada tend to get paid minimum wage, whereas American servers often are paid less in direct wages).

The following tipping guidelines should be considered just that: guidelines. Someone in your party might **tip** a little differently, and this is okay. Tipping is an important North American **social norm** but there's nothing really written in stone, so to speak.
- Tip the pretax amount on your bill, not the taxed amount.
- Tip 15 percent for acceptable service.

> ### The Best Tip Hack Ever
>
> Take your bill. Find the pre-tax total (e.g., $54.79) Move the decimal place over to the left once (e.g., $5.47). Round this number up to the next easy number (e.g., $5.50). This is 10 percent of your bill. Simply double this number to find out what 20 percent of your bill is (e.g., $11.00). You can then simply add this number to your total bill

- Tip 20 percent for great or good service (this is considered a standard tip in most North American restaurants).
- A tip greater than 20 percent would indicate exceptional service, and is something that is obviously appreciated but not expected.

If the service is less than acceptable (for example, if service was slow, rude, or incorrect), you should still tip. Not tipping may make you come off as cheap and careless, or make it seem as if you simply forgot. Instead, consider tipping as little as 5 to 10 percent for poor service. This shows that you made a conscious decision about how much tip to leave, which hopefully will alert the serving staff that something (or several things) they did was not up to standard.

If a restaurant clearly has a sign stating "No tipping," respect the wishes of the establishment and do not try to tip your server.

When settling the bill, tip according to custom. In some countries like America, tipping is virtually mandatory; in others, it's up to the customer's discretion. In some countries tipping is not required at all.

Settling the Check & Tipping

If it is your choice to pay the check by bank card rather than cash, find out beforehand if the restaurant accepts bank cards, and if so, which ones.

Sometimes, your waiter will offer you something for free, such as a round of drinks or an appetizer. Assuming the service was still good to great, you may want to account for this free item when leaving your tip (that is, a free $4 drink won't show up on your bill, but you still may want to leave an extra $1 or $2 on top of the normal tip as a gesture of appreciation).

Make sure you are basing your tip off of the appropriate amount. For instance, if all of you split the price equally between three or four cards, you can simply base your 20 percent tip off the number charged to your debit or credit card, and not the total of the original bill. However, if you used a gift card or certificate, base your tip on the original bill and not the total that remains after the discount has been applied.

In the end, don't let any temporary discomfort discourage you from asking a friend or loved one out for a meal. Sharing food with loved ones can be a highly enjoyable experience and it is a perfect, time-honored way to spend time with people you care about. By being conscious of how you are presenting yourself and making sure that you are acting with good dining etiquette, you can only end up making the experience even better.

Text-Dependent Questions

1. If you're completely dissatisfied with your meal, should you leave a tip? Why or why not? If yes, how much?

2. True or false: on a date, the man should always pay for the meal. Defend your answer.

3. In North America, how much should you typically tip for a dining experience that was good or great?

Research Project

Do some research on social norms relating to tipping in different countries. What's the standard approach to tipping (if any) in countries like France, England, China, and Australia? Write a one- to two-page report about the differences you find around the world.

Series Glossary of Key Terms

appreciation	Gratitude and thankful recognition.
body language	Nonverbal communication through posture or facial expression.
bully	Overbearing person who habitually intimidates weaker or smaller people.
civil	Adhering to the norms of polite social intercourse.
clingy	Tending to stay very close to someone for emotional support.
common sense	Sound judgment based on simple perceptions of a situation.
compatible	Capable of existing together in harmony.
compliment	An expression of affection, respect, or admiration.
confidence	The state of being certain.
cyberbullying	The electronic posting of mean-spirited messages about a person.
empathy	Being aware of the feelings and thoughts of another.
eulogy	A commendatory oration or writing, especially in honor of one deceased.
faux pas	A social blunder.
frenemy	One who pretends to be a friend but is actually an enemy.
gossip	A person who habitually reveals personal facts about others.
grace	Disposition to act with kindness and courtesy.
inappropriate	Not suited for a purpose or situation.
initiative	The power to do something before others do.
inoculation	Injecting a vaccine to protect against or treat disease.
integrity	The quality of being honest and fair.
judgmental	Tending to judge people too quickly and critically.
lust	To have an intense desire or need.
manner	The way something is done or happens.
networking	The cultivation of productive relationships.
peer	One who is of equal standing with another.
poise	A natural, self-confident manner.
polite	Having or showing good manners or respect for others.
prioritize	To organize things so that the most important one is dealt with first.
procrastinate	To put off intentionally and habitually.
problem-solving	The process of finding a solution to a problem.
online	Connected to a computer.
relationship	The way in which two or more people are connected.
respect	To consider worthy of high regard.
RSVP	To respond to an invitation.
self-centered	Concerned solely with one's own needs.
socialize	Participate in social activities.
social media	Forms of electronic communications through which users share information, ideas, and personal messages.
staying power	Capacity of continuing without weakening.
sympathy	Caring about someone else's misfortune or grief.
tact	A keen sense of what to do or say without upsetting other people.

Further Reading

Black, Rebecca. *Dining Etiquette: Essential Guide for Table Manners, Business Meals, Sushi, Wine and Tea Etiquette.* Createspace Independent Publishing, 2014

Post, Lizzie, and Daniel Post Senning. *Emily Post's Etiquette, 19th Edition: Manners for Today.* New York: William Morrow, 2017.

Tower, Jeremiah. *Table Manners: How to Behave in the Modern World and Why Bother.* New York: Farrar, Straus and Giroux, 2016.

Internet Resources

http://emilypost.com This website is home to the work and wisdom of over five generations of Post family etiquette know-how. Learn how to act with grace and class in everything from dining out to sending emails.

https://dineout.nokidhungry.org Find information about this year-round restaurant campaign (as well as participating restaurants near you) to end child hunger by checking the organization's website.

https://etiquetteforeveryday.com/blog/ This website run by professional etiquette coach Kelly Frager offers lots of helpful information and tips on how to have good etiquette in a variety of life circumstances.

Publisher's note:
The websites listed on this page were active at the time of publication. The publisher is not responsible for websites that have changed their addresses or discontinued operation since the date of publication. The publisher will review and update the website list upon each reprint.

Index

Picture Credits

All images in this book are in the public domain or have been supplied under license by © Shutterstock.com. To the best knowledge of the publisher, all images not specifically credited are in the public domain. If any image has been inadvertently uncredited, please notify the publisher, so that credit can be given in future printings.

Video Credits

Page 24 AskMen: http://x-qr.net/1GQd, page 34 The Distilled Man: http://x-qr.net/1D4x, page 42 Howcast: http://x-qr.net/1D42, page 56 Money School: http://x-qr.net/1H86

About the Author

Sarah Smith is a freelance writer currently living and working in the Boston area. She is also a board-certified Doctor of Physical Therapy, licensed by the Commonwealth of Massachusetts. She attended Boston University, where she earned both her doctorate and, as an undergraduate, a bachelor of science in health studies.

Sarah has been writing for her entire life, and first became a published author at age fourteen, when she began contributing to a weekly column for her local newspaper. Since beginning her freelance writing career in earnest in 2014, Sarah has written over 1,500 articles and books. Her work covers a broad range of topics, including psychology and relationships, as well as physical and mental health.

Additionally, she has over fifteen years of professional experience working with typically developing and special-needs children, along with their families, in a variety of settings, including schools, pediatric hospitals, and youth-group fitness programs. She spent over thirteen years working as a private nanny and babysitter for families in both her hometown of Yarmouth, Maine, as well as in and around the great city of Boston. Sarah also has experience tutoring and leading teens and young adults as part of a variety of clinical internship programs for physical therapy.

DATE DUE

LAKE PARK HIGH SCHOOL
RESOURCE CENTER
ROSELLE, IL 60172